I0815547

THE 2010s
THROUGH THE DECADES
BY CHRISTINA LEAF
eureka!
WONDER
SPACEX
#METOO
#TIMESUP

Eureka! books turn real stories into unforgettable experiences. This nonfiction imprint sparks curiosity, encourages critical thinking, and engages middle-grade readers. *Eureka!* books empower young minds to explore the stories of the real world, one fascinating fact at a time. Unravel the power of knowledge and lifelong learning with *Eureka!*

This edition first published in 2026 by Bellwether Media, Inc.

Library of Congress Cataloging-in-Publication Data

LC record for The 2010s available at: https://lccn.loc.gov/2025021819

Editor: Suzane Nguyen Designer: Andrea Schneider

Printed in the United States of America, North Mankato, MN.

TABLE OF CONTENTS

WELCOME TO THE 2010s!

It is a rainy morning in 2016. A girl puts on some leggings and a T-shirt and heads downstairs to eat breakfast. After eating, she takes out her iPad to do homework. The girl asks Alexa to play her studying playlist on the living room Amazon Echo. Her favorite song is "Sorry" by Justin Bieber. After finishing her work, she opens YouTube to watch new videos from her favorite YouTubers. Her sister comes by to show her the latest filters on Snapchat, and they take some silly selfies together to send to friends.

In the afternoon, the sun comes out. The girl puts on her ballet flats and heads out to meet some friends at a frozen yogurt shop. They take pictures of their yogurt, piled high with toppings. Then, they walk around a nearby park catching Pokémon with the *Pokémon Go* app.

That night, the girl's family scrolls through Netflix and picks *Stranger Things* to watch. After the show, she reads a Babysitter's Club book before turning out the light. What a great day in the 2010s!

POKÉMON GO
frozen yogurt

WHAT HAPPENED IN THE 2010s?

The 2010s were a time of turmoil and fighting for change. The **Great Recession** of the late 2000s continued to negatively affect the economy as the 2010s began. High unemployment levels remained as the job market slowly recovered and class **disparities** widened. Many issues also came from the ever-widening political divide. The inability to agree on important topics often led to **stalemates** in the government and rising discontent among people.

Across the globe, people spoke out and rose up in protests, from Occupy **Wall Street** and Black Lives Matter (BLM) in the United States to the Arab Spring across the Middle East. Young people spoke up about improving gun control in the U.S. and fighting **climate change** worldwide. People often addressed frustration and inequality through social media. This allowed protest movements and underrepresented voices to reach a wider audience than ever before.

The internet worked its way further into daily life in other ways, too, from helping a share economy grow to overtaking physical and broadcast media. Media also began to focus on representation as the U.S. population continued to **diversify**. More stories about women, people of color, and the LGBTQ+ community were produced across popular culture. Representation also grew in the business world, as these groups took on more leadership roles in companies.

HOW MUCH?

1 GALLON GAS
$2.79 (2010)
$2.60 (2019)

THE NEW YORK TIMES
(daily national edition in New York)
$3.00 (2010) | $3.00 (2019)

1 GALLON MILK
$3.32 (2010)
$2.90 (2019)

MOVIE TICKET
$7.89 (2010)
$9.16 (2019)

HALF GALLON ICE CREAM
$4.46 (2010)
$4.81 (2019)

2-LITER BOTTLE OF COKE
$1.79 (2010)
$1.55 (2019)

LOAF OF BREAD
$1.36 (2010)
$1.27 (2019)

HISTORY

UNITED STATES HISTORY

On September 17, 2011, a crowd gathered in Lower Manhattan near Wall Street to protest income inequality. People were angry that the economy only benefited the wealthy. They fought for higher wages and against corporate greed. The protests, which became known as Occupy Wall Street, soon spread across the country. The movement put income inequality at the forefront of U.S. politics.

Many violent events cast a shadow over the 2010s. Several schools were rocked by mass shootings. Two of the most notable included Sandy Hook Elementary in Newtown, Connecticut, in 2012 and Marjory Stoneman Douglas High School in Parkland, Florida, in 2018. In 2013, two bombs went off near the finish line of the Boston Marathon. Hundreds of people were injured and three people were killed in the attack. The **terrorist** attack was discovered to be the work of two brothers.

Major weather events also affected the U.S. Deadly tornadoes swept through the Midwest and Southern U.S. in the spring of 2011. In 2012, Hurricane Sandy caused destruction and flooding on the Northeast coast as well as several Caribbean islands.

WE ARE THE 99 PERCENT

Occupy Wall Street protesters used the rallying cry, "We are the 99 percent." This is based on the economy benefitting the top 1 percent of earners.

Deepwater Horizon explosion

OPERATION NEPTUNE SPEAR

In 2011, the U.S. found some justice for the September 11th terrorist attacks after a decade-long hunt. On May 1, U.S. Navy SEAL Team Six conducted Operation Neptune Spear. They flew to a secret compound in Abbottabad, Pakistan. There, they found and killed Osama bin Laden, the leader of the terrorist attacks, as well as several of his associates.

Osama bin Laden

DEEPWATER HORIZON

The oil rig *Deepwater Horizon* exploded on April 20, 2010. Eleven workers were killed, and the rig sank into the Gulf of Mexico. This caused millions of barrels of oil to leak into the water for 87 days, becoming the largest oil spill in history. The disaster caused lasting damage to humans, animals, and the environment.

HURRICANE HARVEY

On August 25, 2017, Hurricane Harvey hit the coast of Texas. It brought with it record-breaking rainstorms. The rainfall led to massive floods. Houston, Texas, was hit the worst. Hurricane Harvey caused $125 billion in damage. It destroyed over 200,000 homes and businesses and killed dozens of people.

flooded streets during Hurricane Harvey

UNITED STATES POLITICS

The U.S. became more and more divided throughout the 2010s. In 2012, Barack Obama defeated Utah Senator Mitt Romney to win a second term as president. However, his administration frequently disagreed with the Republican-led House of Representatives. This made it difficult to pass legislation. In 2013, these disagreements led to the government shutting down for more than two weeks. The problem grew when Republicans won control of the Senate in 2014.

President Barack Obama

ELECTION SHOWDOWN:
2016 PRESIDENTIAL ELECTION

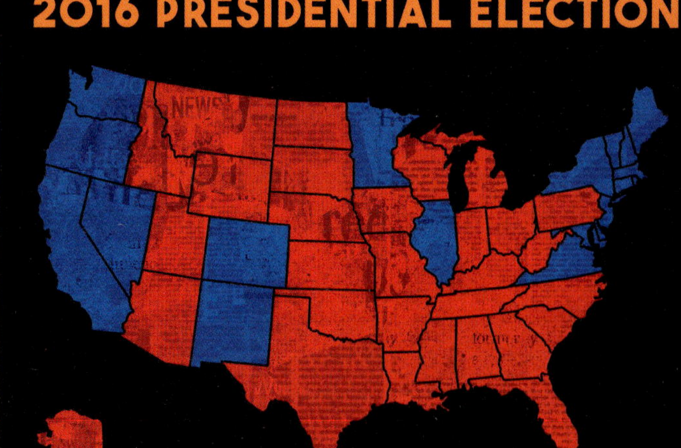

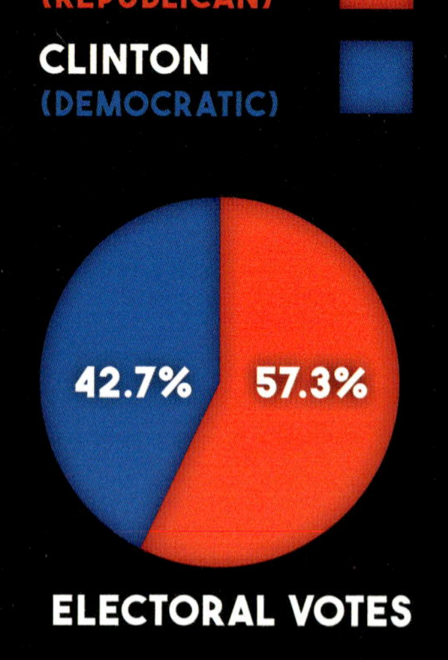

Despite the disagreements, President Obama's administration was still able to make some major changes. In 2010, the Dodd-Frank Act was mandated for financial institutions. Obama also signed the Affordable Care Act, also known as Obamacare, in 2010 to make healthcare accessible and affordable to more people. In 2016, he formally entered the U.S. into the Paris Agreement. This international agreement seeks to limit the impacts of climate change.

The party divide deepened when Donald Trump became president in 2017. Many of his actions reversed acts from the Obama administration, including pulling out of the Paris Agreement and a nuclear agreement with Iran. He also frequently denied facts, made false claims, and said that he did not trust news organizations. Many Republicans began to agree with his ideas. In 2019, the House of Representatives **impeached** President Trump for abuse of power and obstruction of Congress. He was **acquitted** in 2020.

MITT ROMNEY AND BARACK OBAMA'S PRESIDENTIAL DEBATE

PRESIDENT TRUMP BEING SWORN INTO OFFICE

PRESIDENT TRUMP'S IMPEACHMENT HEARING

SPOTLIGHT ON:

THE 2016 PRESIDENTIAL ELECTION

The 2016 presidential election was one for the history books. Democrat Hillary Clinton was the first woman to be the nominated presidential candidate of a major political party. Clinton was named the nominee on July 26, 2016.

On the Republican side, Donald Trump was an unusual candidate with no elected political or military background. His **slogan**, "Make America Great Again," became a unifying force for people who felt that America was no longer a world leader due to foreign influences. Trump was named the nominee on July 19, 2016.

Throughout the campaign, Clinton was hounded by questions about her improper use of her private email server when she was secretary of state. Meanwhile, Trump used **inflammatory** language and made statements that offended people.

Outside influences affected the election as well. An investigation by the Senate after the campaign found that Russian hackers had tried to sway the election toward Trump.

On Election Day, Clinton won the popular vote, but Trump won the **electoral vote**, becoming the 45th president.

MAKING HEADLINES

"Democrats Make Hillary Clinton a Historic Nominee"

—*The New York Times*, July 27, 2016

"DONALD TRUMP IS ELECTED PRESIDENT IN STUNNING REPUDIATION OF THE ESTABLISHMENT"

—*THE NEW YORK TIMES*, NOVEMBER 9, 2016

WHO'S WHO?

HILLARY CLINTON

ROLE:
2016 Democratic Presidential Nominee

KNOWN FOR:
A former secretary of state, senator, and first lady who became the first woman to be the presidential nominee of a major party in the U.S.

DONALD TRUMP

ROLE:
2016 Republican Presidential Nominee

KNOWN FOR:
A businessman in real estate and the star of the reality television show *The Apprentice* who became the 45th President of the U.S.

WORLD HISTORY

The terrorist group Islamic State of Iraq and Syria (ISIS) was a threat for much of the 2010s. ISIS took over parts of Iraq and Syria in 2014. It successfully recruited people over the internet to carry out attacks in other countries, including the U.S. and France. The U.S. led other countries in thousands of attacks against ISIS beginning in 2014. By 2017, ISIS was largely defeated, and it fell completely by 2019.

Armed Russian soldiers entered Ukraine's Crimean Peninsula in early 2014 and quickly **annexed** it. This invasion began the Russo-Ukrainian War. Russia's actions were against international law, so the United Nations (UN) put **sanctions** on Russia. But Crimea remained under Russian control.

In 2016, just over half of British citizens voted to leave the European Union (EU) in a vote called Brexit. Since no country had previously left the EU, leaders struggled to find a path forward. Public support also wavered. However, after nearly four years and several leadership changes, the United Kingdom left the EU on January 31, 2020.

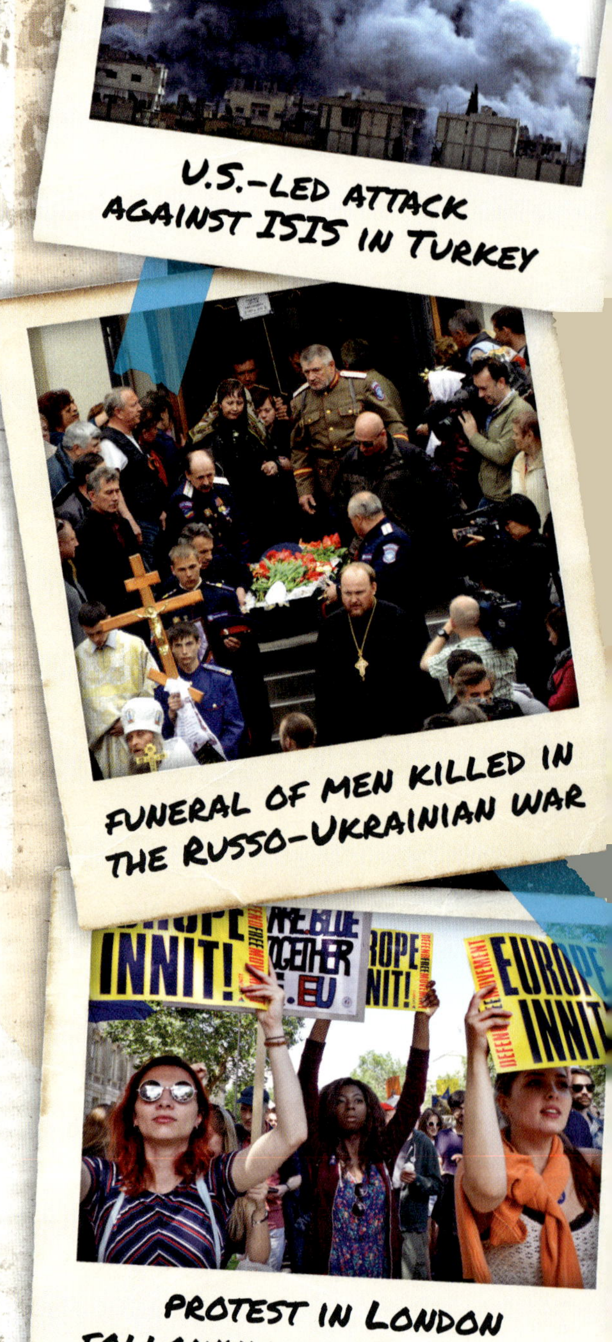

U.S.-LED ATTACK AGAINST ISIS IN TURKEY

FUNERAL OF MEN KILLED IN THE RUSSO-UKRAINIAN WAR

PROTEST IN LONDON FOLLOWING THE BREXIT VOTE

devastation left in Haiti

A NEW VIRUS

In December 2019, some people in Wuhan, China, began having flu-like symptoms due to an unknown illness. This illness soon became known as COVID-19. It would cause a worldwide pandemic beginning in 2020.

HAITIAN EARTHQUAKE

On January 12, 2010, a devastating earthquake rocked Haiti and the Dominican Republic. More than 300,000 people in Haiti were killed in the disaster and around 1.5 million people were left unhoused.

NEW ROYALS

The British royal family expanded in the 2010s. In April 2011, millions of people tuned in to see Prince William marry Kate Middleton. The couple welcomed three children over the next few years. Prince Harry and Meghan Markle were married in May 2018. They have two children. People loved reading about the new generation of royals!

Prince Harry and Meghan Markle's 2018 wedding

Prince William and Kate Middleton's 2011 wedding

SPOTLIGHT ON:

THE ARAB SPRING

In the 2010s, anti-government protests rippled across many northern African and Middle Eastern countries. Many of the countries were led by unfair and controlling leaders. Young citizens called for democracy.

Tunisia was the first country to rise up in protest in December 2010. Shortly after, Egyptians began protesting their president, Hosni Mubarak. Both countries found success with protesting and overthrew their leaders. This inspired citizens in other countries to begin their own revolutions. Some protests were peaceful. But in many places, governments and militaries tried to stop the protests using violence. Protesters also became violent, particularly in Libya, where people formed a **rebellion** against leader Muammar al-Qaddafi.

children protesting Libyan leader Muammar al-Qaddafi

MAKING HEADLINES

"VIOLENT CLASHES MARK PROTESTS AGAINST MUBARAK'S RULE"

—*THE NEW YORK TIMES*, JANUARY 26, 2011

"2011 Person of the Year: The Protester"

—*TIME*, December 26, 2011

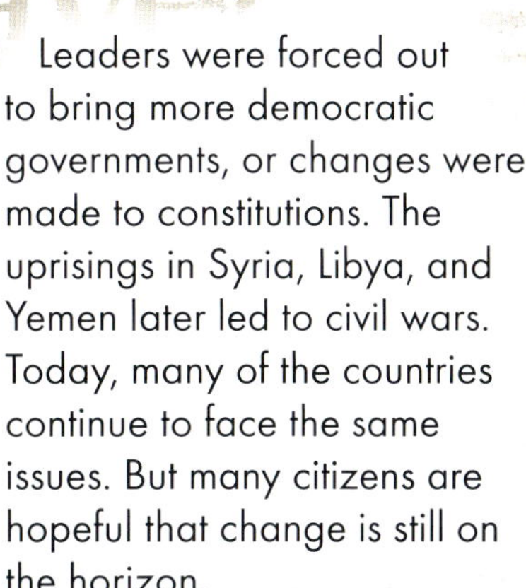

Leaders were forced out to bring more democratic governments, or changes were made to constitutions. The uprisings in Syria, Libya, and Yemen later led to civil wars. Today, many of the countries continue to face the same issues. But many citizens are hopeful that change is still on the horizon.

uprising in Yemen

WHO'S WHO?

ASMAA MAHFOUZ

ROLE:
Egyptian human rights activist

KNOWN FOR:
Posted widely shared social media videos that helped spark the uprising that led to the 2011 Egyptian Revolution

SOCIAL CHANGES

Many major social movements and changes gained traction in the 2010s. LGBTQ+ activists celebrated a major win in the Supreme Court's *Obergefell v. Hodges* case in 2015. This landmark decision legalized same-sex marriages nationwide. Other victories included more LGBTQ+ people in politics, prominent trans people in the media, and the repeal of military bans that prevented LGBTQ+ members from serving openly.

Social media often helped spread awareness for causes. People used #BlackLivesMatter and #BLM to show their anger with how Black people were unjustly treated in society. This started in 2013 after the man who killed unarmed Black teenager Trayvon Martin was acquitted. The movement grew in 2014 after Eric Garner and teen Michael Brown were killed by police officers. Protests followed in Ferguson, Missouri, and across the country. The BLM movement continued to spread as police **brutality** continued.

protester after the acquittal of Trayvon Martin's killer

The end of the decade was marked by the #MeToo movement. Though it had begun years earlier, it exploded in 2017 when actress Alyssa Milano asked women to share stories about workplace **harassment** and abuse on social media. Soon, survivors of abuse and violence came forward to share their experiences.

Jim Obergefell, plaintiff in the *Obergefell v. Hodges* case, at a 2015 Pride Parade

PROTESTERS AFTER MICHAEL BROWN WAS KILLED BY POLICE

PROTESTERS AFTER ERIC GARNER WAS KILLED BY POLICE

ALYSSA MILANO WITH TARANA BURKE, THE FOUNDER OF THE #METOO MOVEMENT

SCIENCE AND TECHNOLOGY

TECHNOLOGY

Artificial intelligence (AI) became more common in everyday life in the 2010s. Siri started as an iPhone app in 2010. This digital assistant listened to users' voices and could set alarms, send messages, or find information. In 2014, Amazon introduced its digital assistant, Alexa, with the Echo speaker. It quickly became even more advanced and could do tasks in the home like turning lights on and off. Other companies soon followed into the digital assistant and smart home market.

AI also brought concerns. Realistic videos of politicians making speeches were later found to be **deepfakes**. People were worried this technology could spread misinformation. Facial recognition, which people can use for security and to unlock smartphones, can also be used for law enforcement surveillance. The technology was also found to be less accurate for racial minorities.

AMAZON ECHO

DEEPFAKE VIDEO OF PRESIDENT OBAMA

Oculus virtual reality headset

The decade brought popular new types of personal technology. The iPad was introduced in early 2010. People loved this easy-to-use tablet! Apple followed up in 2015 with the Apple Watch. Virtual reality headset technology advanced with the Oculus in 2013. The DJI Phantom was also released in 2013. This was one of the first widely available drones for civilian use.

APPS GALORE!

Many popular apps got their start in the 2010s. These include Instagram in 2010, Snapchat in 2011, *Pokémon Go* in 2016, and TikTok in 2018.

SCIENTIFIC DISCOVERIES

Many changes happened in space exploration in the 2010s. NASA launched the last space shuttle, Atlantis, in 2011. But they sent new rovers, Curiosity and Insight, to Mars to continue learning about our neighboring planet. SpaceX furthered its role as a major player in space during the decade. In 2010, SpaceX's Dragon capsule first successfully returned from orbit. SpaceX also successfully reused the Falcon 9 rocket in 2017. In 2019, President Trump formed the Space Force branch of the U.S. military.

SpaceX Dragon capsule

CRISPR-CAS9

WHAT IS IT?:

A technology that can be used to edit genes

INVENTORS:

Jennifer Doudna and Emmanuelle Charpentier

YEAR INVENTED:

2012

EFFECT ON DAILY LIFE:

Among other things, it can be used to detect, treat, and prevent diseases, alter crops to make them better able to grow in harsh conditions, and make farm animals more resistant to diseases.

illustration of an edited gene using CRISPR-Cas9

Spacecrafts such as Voyager and Cassini took new photos of our solar system and beyond. Data from India's Chandrayaan-1 confirmed that there was water ice on Earth's moon in 2018. Scientists also brought us the first photo of a black hole in 2019.

Science made strides on Earth as well. A finger bone found in Russia revealed a new ancestor to today's modern humans. In 2012, the CRISPR-Cas9 system was filed for **patent**. This gene-editing system could alter **DNA**. The FDA approved new medical treatments, such as **gene therapy**. Scientists also continued to warn about the climate crisis, and protesters used their voices to call for action.

JENNIFER DOUDNA AND EMMANUELLE CHARPENTIER

WATER ICE ON EARTH'S MOON DISCOVERED BY CHANDRAYAAN-1

THE FIRST PHOTO OF A BLACK HOLE

Curiosity rover on Mars

DAILY LIFE

LIFE IN THE 2010s

Most Americans lived in urban areas during the 2010s. But **multigenerational** housing grew significantly. The high cost of education and housing drove many young adults to live with their parents to save money.

Hybrid and electric vehicles gained popularity throughout the decade as technology improved and concerns about the environment grew. Smartphones became an essential part of everyday life for many people. Online shopping grew significantly thanks to delivery services like Amazon. This caused many shopping malls to close. Forms of contactless payment like Apple Pay and Venmo also exploded in popularity.

Kids used more technology than ever. Schoolwork was often done on tablets or laptops. Video games and other electronic toys were also popular. Kids still enjoyed playing outside but spent less time outdoors than previous generations.

CHARGING AN ELECTRIC VEHICLE

AMAZON DELIVERY

KIDS DOING SCHOOLWORK ON TABLETS AND LAPTOPS

2010s SLANG

LiT

cool or awesome

FASHION TRENDS

Zendaya

Thanks to the rise of social media, street style fashions such as fanny packs and bomber jackets became more widespread in the 2010s. Influencers shared photos of outfits from their own closets. These posts reached thousands of followers. Fashion also became more inclusive in the decade. Designers began to debut models of all sizes, ages, and races in advertisements and on the runway. The makeup brand CoverGirl signed their first male spokesperson in 2016.

Celebrities and popular culture still sparked trends. For women, Rihanna and Zendaya were known for their bold red carpet looks. New royals Kate Middleton and Meghan Markle inspired sleek, classic looks such as knee-length skirts and neutral color palettes. Skinny jeans, ballet flats, and statement necklaces were hugely popular items among women.

The television show *Mad Men* inspired traditional, slim-fitting suits in menswear in the early part of the decade. Towards the end of the decade, suits became more daring. Men experimented with new colors, patterns, and twists on the standard suit.

One of the biggest daily wear trends was **athleisure**. Women wore leggings and yoga pants for everyday activities. Men sported slim joggers and hoodies. Chunky sneakers were popular.

JAMES CHARLES, COVERGIRL'S FIRST MALE SPOKESPERSON

EXPRESSIVE MENSWEAR SUIT

statement necklace

ATHLEISURE

PRODUCTS AND TOYS

Kids in the 2010s were surrounded by more and more advanced technology. Computers and video games were common throughout the decade. iPads were popular, and smartphones were everywhere. Simpler classic toys such as dolls and stuffed animals continued to be popular as well.

MONSTER HIGH

A new kind of fashion doll emerged in 2010. Monster High dolls dress up classic monsters such as vampires and mummies in stylish outfits with a ghoulish twist. Several movies, a web series, and a book series quickly followed the release of the wildly popular dolls.

NINTENDO SWITCH ↑

Nintendo's Switch console came out in 2017. Its unique technology allowed users to play on the go or connect it to their TV for a bigger screen. Online play allowed for new features in games. New games in popular franchises, such as *The Legend of Zelda: Breath of the Wild* and *Super Mario Odyssey*, also helped sales soar.

MINECRAFT

Minecraft was fully released for computers in 2011. This sandbox video game allows users to create endless worlds, fight mobs, or just explore. It was a huge hit right away! The game's easy gameplay and sense of community made it the best-selling video game of all time!

SPHERO BB-8

Sphero's BB-8 was the hot Christmas gift in 2015. Based on a droid in the popular movie *Star Wars: Episode VII - The Force Awakens*, this toy robot was controlled through an app and voice commands. Users could control its movements, use it to send messages, and even program it to move on its own!

Hatchimal

ROBOT PETS

Kids went wild for electronic pets in the 2010s. Fuzzy hamsters called Zhu Zhu Pets squeaked and moved, while Hatchimals allowed kids to raise toy pets through different stages of life. Fingerlings were toy pets small enough to wrap around a finger!

FUNKO POPS

Toymaker Funko had a hit when they released their signature POPs. These vinyl figurines have big heads and come in many popular characters. A line of superhero-themed POPs debuted at San Diego Comic-Con in 2010. They quickly became a sensation!

FIDGET SPINNERS

For a few months in 2017, fidget spinners were everywhere. These spinning toys were first designed to give people with ADHD and anxiety an outlet for energy and a way to keep calm. The toy's simplicity and classroom bans soon caused interest to wane.

ARTS AND ENTERTAINMENT

PUBLICATIONS

One of the biggest shifts in children's and young adult (YA) literature in the 2010s was the push for diversity in authors and stories. Authors of color, particularly those writing about their own experiences, became more prominent. By the end of the decade, there were more stories about Black and Latino characters than ever before.

E-readers boomed in the early part of the decade, thanks to the popularity of the Amazon Kindle. But print books continued to be the more popular choice. Amazon also had an impact on the decline of chain bookstores such as Barnes & Noble and Borders. These chains could not offer the deals of Amazon or the personal service of independent bookstores.

Audiobooks gained new popularity in the decade as digital versions replaced clunky CD or tape options. Some audiobooks even included full casts for their production! Many magazines and newspapers moved online, offering digital versions of their publications.

READING REC

TITLE:
WONDER

AUTHOR:
R. J. Palacio

YEAR PUBLISHED:
2012

SUMMARY:
Auggie, who has severe facial deformities, struggles with bullies and making friends as he enters fifth grade after a life of being homeschooled.

SOCIAL ISSUES

The decade's focus on social issues was present in its literature as well. *Wonder* became a bestseller early in the decade. Several novels, including the bestseller *The Hate U Give*, told stories about racial injustice. Others, including the popular *Will Grayson, Will Grayson*, featured LGBTQ+ heroes.

DYSTOPIAN NOVELS

The wild popularity of 2008's *The Hunger Games* sparked a demand for YA dystopian novels in the 2010s. *Matched*, *Divergent*, and the Maze Runner series offered postapocalyptic worlds and fearless teen heroes. By the middle of the decade, interest in the genre began to drop off as many books with similar themes and plots flooded the market.

MYTHOLOGY

Mythology retellings continued to sell in children's and YA books thanks to the popularity of Rick Riordan's Percy Jackson and the Olympians series. Riordan wrote new series based on different mythologies, including Egyptian and Norse. Later in the decade, authors wrote series inspired by Hindu, Bengali, West African, Korean, and other mythologies.

Dog Man

GRAPHIC NOVELS

Graphic novels, which had been growing in popularity for decades, enjoyed huge growth in the 2010s. Raina Telgemeier's *Smile* and its sequels were smash hits and helped popularize the medium. Graphic formats helped readers digest complex topics more easily. Series like Dog Man and Diary of a Wimpy Kid flew off shelves. Later, favorite classic books such as *The Giver* and *Pride and Prejudice* were turned into graphic novels.

MOVIES

Streaming services like Netflix and Hulu entered households everywhere during the 2010s after becoming faster and more convenient. The ease and variety offered on streaming services also led to the decline of physical media, such as DVDs and Blu-rays, being sold. People could now digitally rent movies not available on subscription sites for a low price through sites like Amazon.

These changes significantly affected the way people watched movies in several ways. Many streaming services began to produce their own movies. Some earned nominations for major awards. Movies that were produced by streaming services often had shortened runs in theaters, with many going straight to streaming. This led to decreasing numbers of theatergoers.

Lin Manuel-Miranda with other cast members of *Hamilton*

AT THE BOX OFFICE

TOP-GROSSING FILMS OF THE 2010s

- ***Avengers: Endgame*** **(2019)**
- ***Star Wars: Episode VII - The Force Awakens*** **(2015)**
- ***Avengers: Infinity War*** **(2018)**
- ***Jurassic World*** **(2015)**
- ***The Lion King*** **(2019)**
- ***The Avengers*** **(2012)**
- ***Furious 7*** **(2015)**
- ***Frozen II*** **(2019)**
- ***Avengers: Age of Ultron*** **(2015)**
- ***Black Panther*** **(2018)**

The Lion King

Crazy Rich Asians

DISNEY

Disney saw huge numbers at the box office throughout the decade. Their properties, Marvel and Star Wars, put out huge blockbusters that brought millions of fans to theaters. Animated movies under the Disney brand, like *Incredibles 2*, were also major hits. The company also began making live-action remakes of some of their most beloved movies, such as *Beauty and the Beast* and *The Lion King*.

Mr. Incredible

DIVERSITY

The decade began to see diverse new faces in lead roles. Hit movies included *Black Panther* and *Spider-Man: Into the Spider-Verse*. *Crazy Rich Asians* stood out for its majority Asian casting in a major Hollywood film. *Moana* used actors with the same heritage as their characters. Women also began to take the lead in more movies like *Wonder Woman* and *Captain Marvel*.

HAMILTON

In 2015, a new musical called *Hamilton* became a smash hit on Broadway. Creator Lin Manuel-Miranda combined hip-hop and rap with show tunes to tell the story of U.S. Founding Father Alexander Hamilton. The musical broke records at the Tony Awards and won numerous other awards as well.

SUPERHERO MOVIES

Superhero movies were a dominant force in the 2010s, most notably with the Marvel Cinematic Universe (MCU). While this collection of movies began with *Iron Man* in 2008, the release of *The Avengers* in 2012 kicked off the crossover appeal of the MCU. DC soon followed with its own Extended Universe.

The Hulk from *Avengers: Age of Ultron*

TELEVISION

Like with movies, streaming became the dominant way people watched television within the decade. People no longer had to watch shows at the same time that they aired. Platforms often had past seasons of a show available to watch as well. Streaming services also began producing their own shows. Often, all the episodes became available at once. Binge-watching, or watching many or all episodes of a TV season at once, became a common way to watch TV. However, some shows, like the fantasy epic *Game of Thrones*, kept millions of viewers returning weekly for the latest installment.

Podcasts had been around since the early 2000s. But their popularity exploded in 2014. Soon, people were listening to podcasts about news, TV, science, history, and even ones that told ongoing stories.

Cocomelon

TV VS. THE INTERNET

Traditional children's TV programming was reduced in the 2010s due to tough competition from streamers and online platforms like YouTube. This led to many networks and streaming platforms partnering with YouTubers to bring popular brands such as *Ryan's World* and *Cocomelon* onto their channels.

SERIAL AND TRUE CRIME

In 2014, the podcast *Serial* became a sensation. Host Sarah Koenig explored the story of Adnan Syed who had been arrested for murder more than a decade earlier. The weekly show uncovered new angles and allowed listeners to form their own opinions. It even led to Syed's case being reopened. It also sparked a craze for more true crime storytelling across pop culture.

Steven Universe

ANIMATED SHOWS

Despite a difficult market, several animated kids' shows found success in the decade. *Steven Universe* was praised for its representation of LGBTQ+ characters. *The Legend of Korra* continued the story and success of *Avatar: The Last Airbender*. *Gravity Falls* mixed fantastical elements and humor with stories about growing up.

STRANGER THINGS

The fresh storyline of *Stranger Things* had viewers hooked from the first episode. This Netflix original series followed kids as they investigated the disappearance of their friend. The show boosted popularity for things such as '80s fashion and music, Eggo waffles, and the game *Dungeons & Dragons*.

Stranger Things

ADVENTURE TIME

Adventure Time was a popular show for kids and adults alike in the 2010s. This animated show aired on Cartoon Network starting in 2010. It followed a boy named Finn and a shapeshifting dog named Jake. At about 11 minutes per episode, the show packed in wild, fast-paced plots that were often weird and silly but also thoughtful and heartwarming.

MUSIC

Like other forms of media, the biggest change to music in the 2010s was the rise of streaming. Spotify launched in the U.S. in 2011. Other platforms, like Prime Music and Apple Music, soon followed. By 2017, streaming was more popular than physical music. People no longer had to rely on CDs or the radio to listen to new music.

The internet also gave new opportunities to artists. People could access music from other countries more easily. Music such as K-pop and Latin pop gained more popularity in the U.S. Platforms such as YouTube, SoundCloud, and TikTok gave emerging artists like Justin Bieber, Post Malone, and Lil Nas X a starting platform to share their music.

HIP-HOP

After several decades of growing popularity, hip-hop outsold rock and pop to become the most popular genre of the decade. Drake was one of the top-selling artists of the decade, and Kendrick Lamar made albums popular with critics and listeners alike. Cardi B, J Balvin, and Bad Bunny mixed in Latin influences with their hit "I Like It," while Post Malone's music pulled from R&B, country, and grunge.

Kendrick Lamar

2010s PLAYLIST

- ***Despacito***
  Luis Fonsi, Daddy Yankee (2017)
- ***Rolling in the Deep***
  Adele (2010)
- ***Gangnam Style***
  PSY (2012)
- ***Old Town Road***
  Lil Nas X feat. Billy Ray Cyrus (2019)
- ***Shape of You***
  Ed Sheeran (2017)
- ***i***
  Kendrick Lamar (2015)
- ***Formation***
  Beyoncé (2016)
- ***Royals***
  Lorde (2013)
- ***Born This Way***
  Lady Gaga (2011)
- ***7 Rings***
  Ariana Grande (2019)

PSY

COUNTRY

Country music began to split into different directions. Hip-hop influenced the 2019 megahit, "Old Town Road", while artists like Chris Stapleton took inspiration from rock music. Pop influenced many younger country artists, from Taylor Swift early in the decade to Maren Morris later on. Kacey Musgraves leaned into classic country, folk, and pop influences in her 2018 *Golden Hour* album.

Kacey Musgraves

K-POP

In 2012, PSY's "Gangnam Style" took the world by storm. The star's success paved the way for other Korean pop, or K-pop, acts to gain popularity in the U.S. Boy group BTS found success, becoming the first K-pop group to hit number one on the *Billboard* charts. By the end of the decade, girl group BLACKPINK was climbing the *Billboard* charts.

TRAP

Trap hit the mainstream in the 2010s. This genre originated in Southern hip-hop and is known for its hypnotic rhythms, deep bass, and synth beats. Artists such as Waka Flocka Flame and 2 Chainz helped trap gain attention. Soon, similar beats were found in pop songs, like Ariana Grande's "7 Rings." Latin artists like Bad Bunny and Maluma also took to the sound, creating Latin trap.

DANCE POP

Dance pop dominated the charts in the early part of the decade. Hits like Ke$ha's "TiK ToK" and Lady Gaga's "Born This Way" used synth-heavy electronic dance music beats to make upbeat, danceable hits. In 2011, popstar Katy Perry's *Teenage Dream* album became the second album in history to have five number one hit songs.

Lady Gaga

U.S. SPORTS

Football was the most-watched sport in the U.S. in the 2010s. Big games in Major League Baseball (MLB) and the National Basketball Association (NBA) also drew a lot of viewers. Major League Soccer (MLS) continued to expand and gain new fans thanks to the growing popularity of soccer in the U.S. The decade also saw the first game in the National Women's Soccer League (NWSL) in 2013.

Controversy shook sports, too. Scientific studies continued to show evidence of brain damage in many former football players, as well as in other contact sports. MLB was rocked by scandals. In 2013, many players were suspended for using performance-enhancing drugs. At the end of the decade, the Houston Astros were found to be cheating in the 2017 World Series.

MVP

NAME:
LEBRON JAMES

SPORT:
Basketball

YEARS ACTIVE:
2003 to present

TEAMS:
Cleveland Cavaliers, Miami Heat, and Los Angeles Lakers

KNOWN FOR:
One of the greatest basketball players of all time, he played in the NBA Finals every year between 2011 and 2018, with both the Miami Heat and the Cleveland Cavaliers.

ENDING THE CURSE

In 2016, fans went wild when the Chicago Cubs won their first World Series in over 100 years. The team last won in 1908, and some people believed the team was cursed. Game 7 went into extra innings after a brief rain delay. In the 10th inning, the Cubs managed two runs for the win.

THE INTERCEPTION

The New England Patriots played in five Super Bowls in the 2010s. But perhaps the most memorable happened in 2015. The Seattle Seahawks looked poised to score at the one-yard line with 26 seconds left. Instead, Patriots rookie Malcolm Butler intercepted a pass by Seahawks quarterback Russell Wilson. The shocking play sealed the Patriots' fourth Super Bowl win.

WHAT A COMEBACK!

In the 2016 NBA Finals, the Cleveland Cavaliers trailed the Golden State Warriors 3–1. But the Cavaliers stars LeBron James and Kyrie Irving were playing well. The Warriors struggled as players fell to injury and suspension. The Cavaliers won the next three games to take their first-ever NBA championship. This was the biggest Finals series comeback in NBA history!

Colin Kaepernick and Eric Reid

COLIN KAEPERNICK

In 2016, San Francisco 49ers quarterback Colin Kaepernick caused a stir in the National Football League (NFL) and the country. During the national anthem, he chose not to stand. He was protesting police brutality toward Black Americans and unjust treatments of people of color in the country. His teammate, Eric Reid, soon joined him. Kaepernick's protest spread to hundreds of players from other teams and other sports and sparked a national conversation.

GLOBAL SPORTS

Global sports in the 2010s saw several athletes dominate their fields. In the Olympics, Usain Bolt continued his impressive career by taking home six medals in track and field. Michael Phelps and Katie Ledecky ruled men's and women's swimming. Simone Biles dominated the gymnastics world during her debut at the Rio de Janeiro Olympics in 2016. Tennis stars Serena Williams and Novak Djokovic each became the champion of all four major tournaments at one time.

In soccer, Spain won its first ever World Cup in 2010. Germany took home the top prize in 2014, and France came out on top in 2018. The U.S. Women's National Team appeared in all three Women's World Cup finals of the decade, losing to Japan in 2011 but taking home back-to-back wins in 2015 and 2019.

SIMONE BILES

Simone Biles competed at just one Olympics in the 2010s. But it was enough for her to become the decade's most accomplished gymnast. Biles earned 4 gold medals and a bronze at the 2016 Olympics. Biles was undefeated at the World Championships from 2013 to 2019, earning a historic 25 medals. Biles also has several gymnastics moves named after her.

Simone Biles

TENNIS'S BIG THREE

Men's tennis was dominated by players Roger Federer, Rafael Nadal, and Novak Djokovic during the 2010s. These three often traded top rankings, Grand Slam wins, and Masters titles throughout the decade. Out of the 40 Grand Slam titles in the decade, they won 33. Their tough competition brought excitement to fans and elevated the sport.

A BIG LOSS

One of the most stunning World Cup games happened in 2014. Brazil faced Germany in the semi-finals. Brazil, who remained undefeated, hoped to reach the final in their home country. But Germany shockingly scored five goals in the first 30 minutes. Two more goals followed in the second half. Brazil scored in the 90th minute of the game, but it was still the country's biggest defeat since 1920.

PERFORMANCE-ENHANCED RUSSIA

Russia hosted its first Winter Olympics in 2014. The country more than doubled the number of medals it won since the previous Olympics. Investigations after the Games found that the Russian government had encouraged its athletes to take illegal performance-enhancing drugs. The International Olympic Committee decided to ban Russia from the 2018 Games but allowed Russian athletes who passed drug tests to compete. The ban continued into the 2020s and extended to other sports competitions as well.

CHLOE KIM →

The decade saw a young star emerge in snowboarder Chloe Kim. In 2015, she won the X Games superpipe competition at age 14. She was the youngest person ever to accomplish this! The next year, Kim became the first woman to land two back-to-back **1080s**. At PyeongChang in 2018, she became the youngest female snowboarder to win a gold medal in the halfpipe.

Chloe Kim

TIMELINE

JANUARY 12, 2010
A major earthquake destroys much of Haiti

DECEMBER 17, 2010
Tunisia rises up against its government, sparking a wave of revolts known as the Arab Spring

MAY 2, 2011
SEAL Team Six completes Operation Neptune Spear, killing Osama bin Laden

JULY 8, 2011
NASA launches Atlantis, the last space shuttle

JULY 14, 2011
Spotify launches in the U.S.

SEPTEMBER 17, 2011
People gather near Wall Street to protest inequality in the start of Occupy Wall Street

MAY 4, 2012
The Avengers hits theaters

JULY 15, 2012
The music video for "Gangnam Style" is released on YouTube

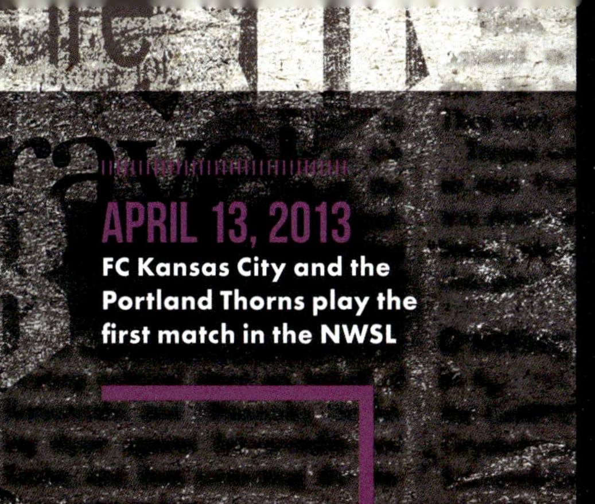

APRIL 13, 2013

FC Kansas City and the Portland Thorns play the first match in the NWSL

JULY 13, 2013

The man who killed unarmed Black teenager Trayvon Martin is acquitted, sparking the Black Lives Matter movement

OCTOBER 29, 2012

Hurricane Sandy hits the Atlantic coast

OCTOBER 3, 2014

The first episode of the podcast *Serial* is released

APRIL 15, 2013

Two bombs explode in the crowd of spectators watching the Boston Marathon

FEBRUARY 20, 2014

Armed Russian soldiers enter the Crimean Peninsula and take control

DECEMBER 12, 2012

CRISPR-Cas9 technology is filed for patent

JUNE 26, 2015
The Supreme Court rules that states must recognize same-sex marriage in *Obergefell v. Hodges*

AUGUST 6, 2015
Hamilton premieres on Broadway

JUNE 23, 2016
The United Kingdom votes to leave the European Union in a move known as Brexit

JULY 26, 2016
Hillary Clinton is the first woman to become the presidential nominee of a major U.S. political party

AUGUST 29, 2016
President Barack Obama signs an order to formally enter the U.S. into the Paris Agreement

NOVEMBER 2, 2016
The Chicago Cubs win their first World Series in 108 years

NOVEMBER 8, 2016
Donald Trump is elected president of the U.S.

MARCH 3, 2017
The Nintendo Switch is released worldwide

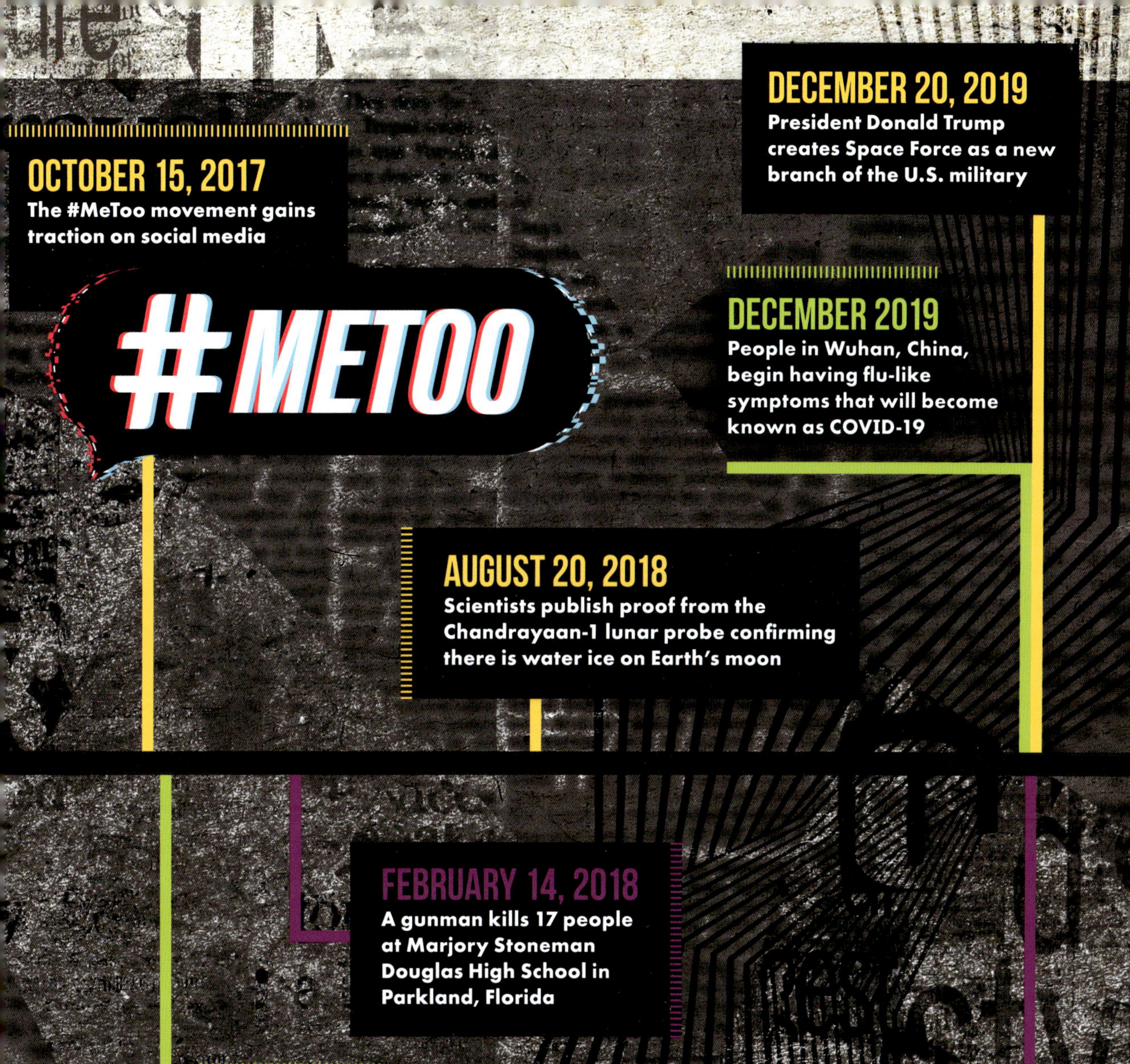

OCTOBER 15, 2017
The #MeToo movement gains traction on social media

DECEMBER 20, 2019
President Donald Trump creates Space Force as a new branch of the U.S. military

DECEMBER 2019
People in Wuhan, China, begin having flu-like symptoms that will become known as COVID-19

AUGUST 20, 2018
Scientists publish proof from the Chandrayaan-1 lunar probe confirming there is water ice on Earth's moon

FEBRUARY 14, 2018
A gunman kills 17 people at Marjory Stoneman Douglas High School in Parkland, Florida

NOVEMBER 1, 2017
The Houston Astros beat the Los Angeles Dodgers in the World Series but are later found to have cheated

DECEMBER 18, 2019
The House of Representatives impeaches Donald Trump for abuse of power

GLOSSARY

1080s—snowboarding moves in which a person makes three full turns in the air

acquitted—declared innocent of a crime or wrongdoing

annexed—added to one's own territory to form a large country

artificial intelligence—the ability of computers to mimic human behavior

athleisure—casual clothing that can be worn for working out or daily life

brutality—cruel or harsh treatment

climate change—a human-caused change in Earth's weather due to warming temperatures

deepfakes—images or videos that have been changed to show people saying or doing things that did not happen

disparities—often obvious differences between two things

diversify—to be made up of people from many different backgrounds

DNA—a tiny substance that carries information about the makeup of a living thing

electoral vote—a tally of the votes cast by the electoral college; the electoral college is a group of electors that select the president and vice president of the United States; in the electoral college, each state gets a number of electoral votes based on the amount of members of Congress it has.

gene therapy—a specialized treatment of illnesses or disorders where modified genes are inserted to replace problematic genes

genre—a category of a kind of art based on style, form, or content

Great Recession—a global economic downturn in the late 2000s that had a slow recovery

harassment—the act of creating an unpleasant situation with unwelcome verbal or physical behavior

hybrid—able to use both a gasoline engine and an electric motor

impeached—charged a public official with a crime done while in office

inflammatory—provoking anger, excitement, or an uproar

LGBTQ+—a community of people who identify as something other than heterosexual or the gender they were assigned at birth; LGBTQ+ stands for Lesbian, Gay, Bisexual, Transgender, Queer and other identities.

multigenerational—relating to more than one generation

patent—an official document or license granting a right for a person or company to be the only seller, maker, or user of an invention

rebellion—a series of actions that are opposed to authority or the government

sanctions—economic or military actions by countries to force another country to stop breaking international laws

sandbox—relating to a kind of game that allows players to endlessly build and create things without limits

slogan—relating to a catchy phrase used for advertising

stalemates—states of inaction in which neither party is willing to move or compromise

synth—related to a musical instrument called a synthesizer; a synthesizer can produce a wide variety of sounds.

terrorist—related to a person who uses fear to try to control others

Wall Street—a financial district in New York City that represents the powerful financial interests that control or influence the U.S. economy

WRITE ABOUT IT!

- Are there any events from the 2010s that continue to affect life today? **What are they?**
- **How** has technology changed from the 2010s to today?
- If you could experience any event from the 2010s, what would it be? **Why?**

ALSO CHECK OUT

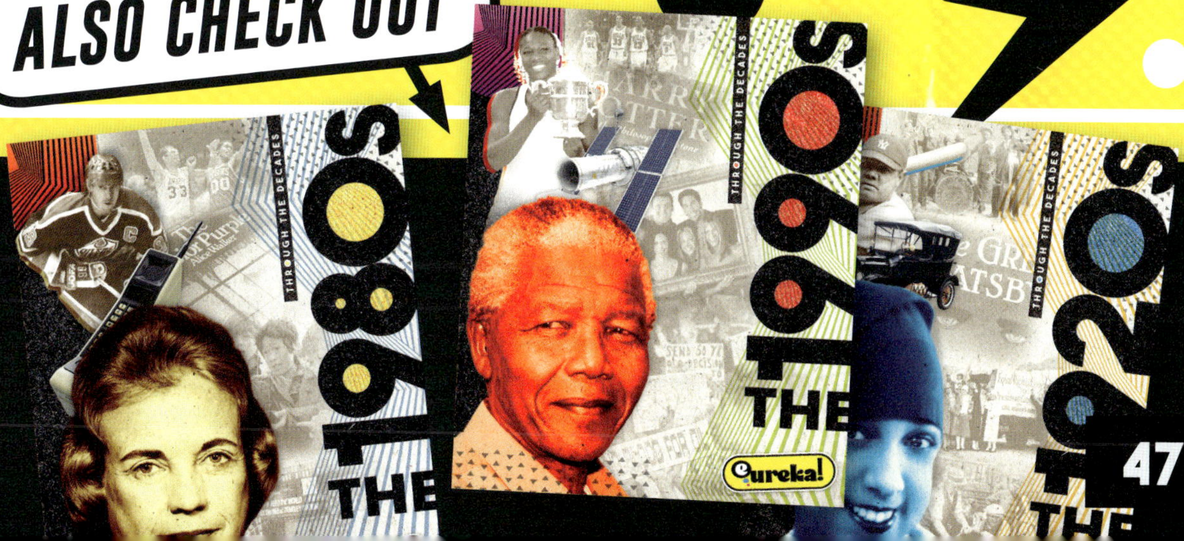

THROUGH THE DECADES
THE 1980s

THROUGH THE DECADES
THE 1990s
Eureka!

THROUGH THE DECADES
THE 1920s

INDEX

The images in this book are reproduced through the courtesy of: Joe Seer, front cover (Trump); NASA Johnson Space Center/ Wikipedia, front cover (CRS-20 Dragon), p. 21 (CRS-20 Dragon); Focus Pix, front cover (Biles); Sundry Photography, front cover (protest); Photo 12/ Alamy Stock Photo, front cover (Black Panther); booksR/ Alamy Stock Photo, front cover (Wonder), p. 30 (Wonder); Aflo Co. Ltd./ Alamy Stock Photo, front cover (MLB), p. 39 (MLB); Album/ Alamy Stock Photo, pp. 3 (Adventure Time), 33 (Mr. Incredible), 35 (Adventure Time); WPA Pool/ Pool/ Getty Images, pp. 3 (wedding), 15 (wedding); Tribune Content Agency LLC/ Alamy Stock Photo, pp. 3 (Kaepernick), 39 (Kaepernick); Sanja Bucko/ Warner Bros/ Kobal/ Shutterstock, pp. 3 (Crazy Rich Asians), 33 (Crazy Rich Asians); Gillian Pullinger/ Alamy Stock Photo, p. 4 (The Babysitter's Club); Frmorrison/ Wikipedia, p. 4 (Amazon Echo); Aleksey Popov | Dreamstime.com, p. 4 (Snapchat filter); Delpixart/ Getty Images, p. 5 (Pokémon Go); antoniodiaz, p. 5 (yogurt); SOPA Images Limited/ Alamy Stock Photo, p. 6; Winai Tepsuttinun, p. 7 (gas); Artiom Photo, p. 7 (milk); Photo Builder, p. 7 (newspaper); phive2015, p. 7 (bread); AlenKadr, p. 7 (Coke); Simon Dack/ Alamy Stock Photo, p. 8; U.S. Coast Guard/ Handout/ Getty Images, p. 9 (explosion); Getty Images/ Staff/ Getty Images, p. 9 (bin Laden); Eric Overton, p. 9 (Harvey); Pictorial Press Ltd/ Alamy Stock Photo, p. 10; Brooks Kraft/ Contributor/ Getty Images, p. 11 (debate); Chip Somodevilla/ Staff/ Getty Images, p. 11 (office); Pool/ Pool/ Getty Images, p. 11 (hearing); AlexCorv/ Alamy Stock Photo, p. 11 (sign); UPI/ Alamy Stock Photo, pp. 13 (Clinton), 40 (Winter 2010); Everett Collection Inc/ Alamy Stock Photo, p. 13 (Trump); Anadolu/ Contributor/ Getty Images, pp. 14 (Turkey), 23 (rover); KIRILL KUDRYAVTSEV/ Contributor/ Getty Images, p. 14 (funeral); Janine Wiedel Photolibrary/ Alamy Stock Photo, p. 14 (protest); Leah Gordon, p. 15 (Haiti); boonchai wedmakawand/ Getty Images, p. 15 (virus); Chris Jackson/ Staff/ Getty Images, p. 15 (William and Kate); Getty Images/ Stringer/ Getty Images, p. 16; MOHAMMED HUWAIS/ Stringer/ Getty Images, p. 17 (Yemen); FREDERICK FLORIN/ Staff/ Getty Images, p. 17 (Mahfouz); Cal Sport Media/ Alamy Stock Photo, p. 18 (sign); Ted Soqui/ Contributor/ Getty Images, p. 18 (protester); Marcus Yam/ Contributor/ Getty Images, p. 19 (Obergefell); Scott Olson/ Staff/ Getty Images, p. 19 (Brown protesters); SEAN DRAKES/ Alamy Stock Photo, p. 19 (Garner protesters); Desiree Navarro/ Contributor/ Getty Images, p. 19 (Milano and Tarana); Bloomberg/ Contributor/ Getty Images, pp. 20 (Echo), 21; ASSOCIATED PRESS/ AP Newsroom, p. 20 (deepfake); Science Photo Library/ Alamy Stock Photo, p. 22 (gene); picture alliance/ Contributor/ Getty Images, p. 23 (Doudna and Charpentier); World History Archive/ Alamy Stock Photo, p. 23 (water ice); Xinhua/ Alamy Stock Photo, p. 23 (black hole); Marc Bruxelle, p. 24 (vehicle); Hadrian, p. 24 (Amazon); WBMUL, p. 24 (kids); Neilson Barnard/ Staff/ Getty Images, p. 26; Everett Collection, p. 27 (necklace); Fairfax Media/ Contributor/ Getty Images, p. 27 (Charles); LISA O'CONNOR/ Contributor/ Getty Images, p. 27 (suit); Sv Svetlana, p. 27 (athleisure); Evan-Amos/ Wikipedia, pp. 28 (Switch), 44 (March 2017); Gareth Cattermole/ Staff/ Getty Images, p. 28 (Monster High); PA Images/ Alamy Stock Photo, p. 29 (Hatchimal); jpgfactory, p. 29 (Sphero BB-8); Stefan Lambauer, p. 29 (Funko); Patti McConville/ Alamy Stock Photo, p. 31 (The Hate U Give); Jeff Whyte, p. 31 (Dog Man); Bruce Glikas/ Contributor/ Getty Images, p. 32 (Hamilton); Entertainment Pictures/ Alamy Stock Photo, pp. 32 (The Lion King), 33 (The Hulk); ©Netflix/ Courtesy Everett Collection, pp. 34 (Cocomelon), 35 (Stranger Things); John B Hewitt/ Alamy Stock Photo, p. 34 (Serial); ©Cartoon Network/ Courtesy: Everett Collections, p. 35 (Steven Universe); MediaPunch Inc/ Alamy Stock Photo, p. 36; Francis Specker/ Alamy Stock Photo, p. 37 (PSY); Adam McCullough, p. 37 (Musgraves); s_bukley, p. 37 (Gaga); Eric Gay/ ASSOCIATED PRESS/ AP Newsroom, p. 38; Ian MacNicol/ Contributor/ Getty Images, p. 40 (Summer 2012); Foto Arena LTDA/ Alamy Stock Photo, p. 40 (Summer 2016); CTK/ Alamy Stock Photo, p. 40 (Winter 2014); Jamie Squire/ Staff/ Getty Images, p. 40 (Winter 2018); PCN Photography/ Alamy Stock Photo, p. 41 (all); Carolina K. Smith MD, p. 42 (May 2011); Rawpixel.com, p. 42 (July 2011); Cinematic/ Alamy Stock Photo, p. 42 (May 2012); Roberto Gonzalez/ Stringer, p. 43 (July 2013); Karla Coté/ SOPA Images/ Shutterstock, p. 43 (February 2014); rudy k/ Alamy Stock Photo, p. 44 (June 2015); HOW HWEE YOUNG/ Stringer/ Getty Images, p. 44 (August 2016); Bruce Leighty/ Alamy Stock Photo, p. 44 (November 2016); Geopix/ Alamy Stock Photo, p. 44 (December 2019).